PIONEERS OF SCIENCE

THOMAS EDISON

Nina Morgan

Wayland

Pioneers of Science

Archimedes
Alexander Graham Bell
Karl Benz
Marie Curie
Thomas Edison
Albert Einstein
Michael Faraday
Galileo
Guglielmo Marconi
Isaac Newton
Louis Pasteur
Leonardo da Vinci

Book editor Paul Bennett
Series editor Rosemary Ashley
Designer David Armitage

First published in 1991 by
Wayland (Publishers) Limited
61 Western Road, Hove
East Sussex BN3 1JD, England

British Library Cataloguing in Publication Data
Morgan, Nina
  Thomas Edison.
  1. Electrical engineering. Edison, Thomas A. (Thomas Alva)
  1847–1931
  I. Title   II. Series
  621.3092

  ISBN 0–7502–0164–9

Typeset by DP Press, Sevenoaks
Printed in Italy by Rotolito Lombardo S.p.A.
Bound in France by A.G.M.

Contents

When Thomas Alva Edison was born on 11 February 1847, the USA was still less than 100 years old, and was a very different place than it is now. In those early days, families 'went west' in covered wagons in search of their fortunes. But young Edison eventually made his fortune by travelling east, to the great cities of Boston and New York.

When Edison was born, the atmosphere in the USA seemed to buzz with creative energy. Coming up with new inventions was a national pastime. Many people joked that the first thing a typical American baby did when placed in its cradle was to examine it to see what improvements could be made!

Just as it is today, New York in the 1870s was a bustling centre of business and opportunity.

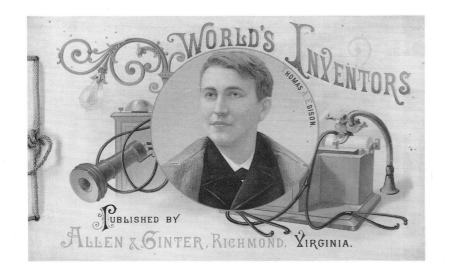

The young inventor pictured on the cover of a book about the world's inventors.

Edison thrived in this environment, because inventing was what he liked to do best. He had a remarkable ability to recognize a mechanical problem and devise a brilliant solution to it. Later in life, he listed his interests as 'everything', and everything describes the scope of his work: he started by working on improvements to the telegraph and went on to produce more than a thousand inventions. He applied for so many patents that people said he kept the path to the Patent Office hot with his footsteps.

'The point in which I am different from most inventors,' he once said, 'is that I have, besides the usual inventor's make-up, a bump of practicality as a sort of appendix, the sense of the business, money value of an invention.' And this 'bump of practicality' led Edison to invent the gramophone, the type of telephone we use today, an improved telegraph system, the cine-camera and electric lights. He aimed to produce one minor invention every ten days, and one major one every six months. By the end of his life he had applied for over 1,300 patents, and was one of the most successful inventors of all time. The boy his teachers described as 'addled' grew up to become 'the man who invented the future'.

The familiar electric light bulb. Thanks to the genius of Thomas Edison, our homes, streets and schools are bright with electric lighting.

The Young Entrepreneur

Thomas Alva Edison, known to all his friends as Al, was the youngest child of Samuel and Nancy Edison. The Edisons lived in the quiet, peaceful town of Milan, Ohio in the American mid-west. But Milan was not quite so peaceful after Al was born, because the youngest Edison boy had a real spirit of adventure and got into many scrapes.

As soon as he could talk, Al started asking questions. Why is the sky blue? Where do the canal boats go? Although Al's brothers and sisters were many years older than he was, Al was never lonely. Samuel Edison owned a timberyard and Al spent hours there building things with scraps of wood, drawing pictures and conducting 'experiments'.

Al's father, Samuel, allowed him to conduct experiments in his timber yard. His mother, Nancy, stood up for him when his teacher said he was 'addled'.

Al loved experimenting. Once he burned down a barn in the course of an experiment to see what fire could do. His father was very angry and punished Al by whipping him in public. But although his father's blows made him cry, they did not dampen Al's sense of curiosity.

When Al was seven, his family moved to Port Huron, Michigan, 160 km north of Milan. The next year, Al started at the local school, but his school career was very short. After three months Al came home and told his mother that the teacher had called him 'addled', and thought that he was a backward boy who could not learn. Nancy Edison was very angry. She told the teacher he did not know what he was talking about, and from then on taught her son at home. Young Al never forgot the way his mother stood up for him, and he always worked hard to be worthy of her.

Benjamin Franklin (1706–90) flying a kite in an electrical storm. Franklin's experiments with electricity inspired Edison to do his own research into electricity.

Alphabet		
A ●▬	J ●▬▬▬	S ●●●
B ▬●●●	K ▬●▬	T ▬
C ▬●▬●	L ●▬●●	U ●●▬
D ▬●●	M ▬▬	V ●●●▬
E ●	N ▬●	W ●▬▬
F ●●▬●	O ▬▬▬	X ▬●●▬
G ▬▬●	P ●▬▬●	Y ▬●▬▬
H ●●●●	Q ▬▬●▬	Z ▬▬●●
I ●●	R ●▬●	

Numerals

1 ●▬▬▬▬	6 ▬●●●●	
2 ●●▬▬▬	7 ▬▬●●●	
3 ●●●▬▬	8 ▬▬▬●●	
4 ●●●●▬	9 ▬▬▬▬●	
5 ●●●●●	0 ▬▬▬▬▬	

Punctuation and other signs

●▬●▬●▬	▬●▬●▬●	●▬●▬●
Period	Semicolon	End of message
▬▬▬●●●	●▬●●▬●	●▬●●●
Colon	Quotation marks	Wait
▬▬●●▬▬	▬●▬	●▬●
Comma	Start	Understand

In Morse code, the letters of the alphabet, numbers and punctuation are represented by different patterns of dots and dashes. These can be transmitted over wires by long and short pulses of electricity.

Al loved his lessons at home and learned quickly. He was especially interested in science. By the time he was ten, he had set up his own laboratory in the basement of his parents' house. He devoted all his spare time to conducting chemistry experiments and, although Nancy was happy to see her son so interested and content, she was not pleased when Al's chemistry experiments produced bad smells, burnt clothing, or ruined furniture.

Al was also very interested in electricity. After reading how the American inventor and statesman, Benjamin Franklin, had conducted experiments with electricity, Al decided to do some himself. He began by attaching the tails of two tom cats to wires, and then rubbing their fur to create static electricity. The main result of this experiment was two very angry cats, and some deep scratches on Al's body.

Al's interest in electricity led to his fascination with the telegraph, a machine that transmitted messages over a distance using electrical impulses sent along wires. The messages were tapped out by operators using Morse code, a code in which letters are represented by combinations of dots and dashes, or short and long pulses of electric current. Al soon rigged up a homemade telegraph so that he could send messages to a friend.

When Al was twelve, the great steam-powered 'iron horse', or railroad, reached Port Huron – an event which was to change Al's life. With his father's blessing, he applied for a job as a newsboy on the train. All day long Al rode on the train between Port Huron and Detroit, selling newspapers and refreshments to the travellers. It was hard work, but Al loved the railway life and made the most of his opportunities. He got permission to set up a small chemistry laboratory in the corner of a baggage car, and continued his experiments in his spare time. He also spent hours watching the station telegraph operators tap out messages in Morse code and decided that he would like to become a telegrapher.

In the nineteenth century, the telegraph was an important means of communication, and in America the transmission lines often ran alongside the railway track. Al spent hours watching the station telegraph operators tap out messages in Morse code, and decided that he, too, would like to become a telegrapher.

Al was given permission to set up a small chemistry laboratory in the corner of a baggage car. Not all of his experiments were successful!

While he was working on the trains, Al suddenly lost his hearing, possibly as a result of having had scarlet fever as a child, or perhaps due to hitting his head. But Al made the most of his handicap. He developed a liking for his own company, an awareness of human nature, and great powers of concentration. In spite of his near deafness, Al was determined to succeed in the world by his wits.

Al enjoyed his life on the trains, and devised many clever ways to sell more newspapers and make more money. But his true love was the telegraph. When he was fifteen, Al rescued the telegraph operator's small son from a moving freight car and as a reward the operator offered to teach Al all about telegraphy. Al learned quickly, and within a few weeks he was as expert as his teacher.

By the time he was sixteen, Al was ready for his first job as an operator. The Civil War was being fought and telegraph operators were in great demand. Later in life, Edison said that thanks to telegraphy he never had to worry if an invention failed. He could always earn enough to live on by operating a telegraph.

When Al was twelve, he got a job as a newsboy on the train that ran between Port Huron and Detroit.

Edison's first telegraphy job was as an operator in the local Port Huron telegraph office. Although the office was not a very busy one, outgoing messages sometimes accumulated while Al worked on his chemical experiments, or read his favourite magazine, *Scientific American*.

In 1863, when Al was sixteen, he got his first job as a railway telegrapher, working as a night operator at Stratford Junction in Ontario, Canada. Again, the office was not busy, so Edison took to spending much of his time on experiments. This led to his first practical invention, a device to send a message automatically.

Night telegraph operators were required to send a signal each hour to the train dispatcher to show that they were still awake. After a long day experimenting, Edison was too tired to stay awake at night. Instead of sleeping more during the day, he decided to invent a clockwork device that automatically sent the necessary signal each hour. This worked well for a while, but eventually he was caught out when a train message sent to him immediately after his hourly signal brought no response. His employer may have appreciated the cleverness of his invention, but Al lost his job.

While still working as a newsboy, Al set up a small printing press on the train and published a weekly paper, The Weekly Herald, *for the other railway employees.*

A report in a French magazine credited Edison with inventing a telephone system that could be used in moving trains. Here a telegrapher is shown, using the telephone to receive a message while sitting in a railway carriage.

No matter how many jobs he lost, Al always found another one. Whenever possible he chose to work nights, so that his days were free for experimenting. For the next five years, he roved the American mid-west as a telegrapher, but his main interest was inventing. He never cared where he lived, or what he ate, or how he dressed. All his spare money went to buy supplies for his experiments.

In 1868, when he was twenty-one, Edison decided to try his luck on the east coast of America. He headed for Boston, where his unfashionable clothes and mid-western accent made him feel out of place. He soon met up with one of his telegrapher friends and together they moved into a boarding house. Edison found a job as a night operator in the Boston office of the powerful Western Union Telegraph Company.

Michael Faraday (1791–1867) was a British scientist who was famous for his work with electricity and magnetism. Faraday's book, Experimental Researches in Electricity, *was a great inspiration to the young Edison.*

Not long after he started at Western Union, Edison came across the book *Experimental Researches in Electricity* by Michael Faraday, the British scientist famous for his work with electricity. This book changed Edison's life. His boarding house room was soon filled with a tangled mass of assorted wires, metals and chemicals. He fell back into his old habits – working by night, and experimenting and inventing by day.

The Young Inventor

After he arrived in Boston, Edison once again began to dream up new inventions. He was always busy and once said to his room-mate, 'I have got so much to do and life is so short, I am going to hustle.'

He had much to inspire him. Boston was a haven for would-be inventors. Many science addicts spent their days in a shop in Court Street owned by Charles Williams Jr. Edison visited the shop often, and was greatly stimulated by the people he met there. By June 1868, he had devised an 'interesting, simple and ingenious' duplex telegraph, which could send two messages, travelling in opposite directions, down the wire at the same time. He also worked on a mechanical stock ticker, a device for relaying the latest stock prices to businessmen in their offices.

A view of Boston in the mid-1800s. When Edison arrived in Boston in 1868, it was an important centre of shipping, commerce and learning, just as it is today.

A diagram of Edison's first patented invention, the electrical vote recorder. The machine worked well but, unfortunately, nobody wanted it!

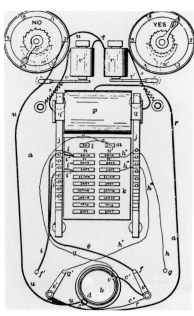

His duplex telegraph attracted some interest, and Edison was lucky enough to convince a Boston businessman to give him $500 to continue his work, in exchange for a half share in any future profits from the invention. On the strength of this, Edison resigned from his job at Western Union and set up on his own as an independent inventor.

Edison could now concentrate on his talent for recognizing a need and inventing an ingenious way of satisfying it. He soon came up with a brilliant idea for a machine that would automatically record the votes of the Representatives in the American Congress, using an electromagnetic impulse. He worked hard on his clever and useful invention, which became the subject of his first patent, granted in June 1869. But, unfortunately, it was an invention that nobody wanted. Edison emerged from this episode a sadder, but wiser, man. From then on, he decided to restrict his efforts to inventing products that people would want and that would sell.

Edison's second patent was for an automatic stock ticker. This invention was more successful and he persuaded thirty subscribers to rent a machine from him. But Edison soon fell out with his backers, and decided to leave Boston and try his luck in New York.

He arrived penniless in New York in the summer of 1869, with no job and nowhere to stay. The first night he spent wandering the streets until dawn. On the second day, he decided to call on Franklin Pope, who was the chief engineer at the Laws Gold Indicator Company. Pope had heard of Edison's inventions and offered him encouragement.

Unfortunately, there were no jobs available in the company, but Pope offered to let Edison sleep in his office until he found a place to live. Edison leapt at the opportunity, and set about finding out

The printing telegraph became indispensable for transmitting information between city offices.

all he could about how the gold indicator worked. The gold indicator was a system for transmitting minute-by-minute information about gold prices into dealers' offices all over the city. One day, a part in the transmitter broke down. Edison spotted the cause of the fault and quickly mended the apparatus. As a result, he was offered a job at a salary of $300 a month, a real fortune!

All summer Edison worked hard at the Laws Gold Indicator Company, adapting, inventing and designing new machines. In the autumn he decided to leave the company and set up in partnership with Pope and another man. They called their venture, Pope, Edison and Company, Electrical Engineers and General Telegraphic Agency. This was the first electrical engineering company in the USA.

17

All through the autumn and winter, Edison worked on a new type of printing telegraph to report gold prices. His device was so successful that it threatened Western Union's business. To prevent this, Western Union offered to buy Edison's gold printer for $15,000. This was a fortune to Edison, but he had to share it with his two partners, even though he had done all of the work on the device.

This experience convinced Edison that it was better to work on his own, and in June 1870 he left the partnership to set up his own business. One of his first customers was the head of Western Union, General Lefferts, who had been impressed by Edison's work on the gold printer. He offered

Edison the chance to work independently on improvements to the Western Union system, and to be paid separately for each invention. Edison happily agreed, even though he had no idea how much he would earn.

After he had produced a series of minor improvements, Western Union asked Edison to try to solve a problem which caused its machines to start printing nonsense. Edison came up with the solution in about three weeks, and his invention was so advanced that it made all other machines seem old-fashioned.

When General Lefferts asked how much he thought his work was worth, Edison asked General Lefferts to make him an offer – he secretly hoped for $5,000, but hardly dared to ask for so great an amount of money. Edison was amazed when General Lefferts asked him if he thought $40,000 would be a fair payment!

General Lefferts, the head of the powerful Western Union Telegraph Company. Lefferts was impressed with Edison's gold printer and asked him to work on improvements to Western Union's telegraphs.

5 The Wizard's Laboratory

The $40,000 gave Edison the chance to set up his own laboratory. In the winter of 1871, he rented the top floor of a three-storey building in nearby Newark, New Jersey. Western Union gave Edison an order for 1,200 new stock tickers, worth nearly half a million dollars, and the future looked very bright indeed.

Just one month later, Edison had spent all the money on equipment. But he was sure he could earn more, and happily wrote to his parents that he was 'a bloated Eastern manufacturer'. He offered to send them money whenever they needed it.

When hiring workers for his new laboratory, Edison looked for men who were skilled craftsmen and had 'light fingers'. Most of his workers had been trained as clockmakers and machinists. Some of the most skilled craftsmen of the time came to work for Edison at Newark. One of his employees, Johann Schuckert, later returned to his native Germany and became one of the founders of the huge German electrical manufacturer, Siemens.

Edison kept his men working long hours. When all seemed to be going pretty smoothly, Edison used to say 'Well, boys, now let's find the bugs.' Once when Edison was having trouble with a large order of stock tickers, he locked his assistants in the laboratory for sixty hours, until he was satisfied that all the 'bugs' were removed, and every detail was right.

No matter how hard his men worked, Edison always worked harder and won the respect and admiration of his crew. The men knew that life in

Edison (centre) with some of his assistants.

the Newark workshop might be demanding, but it was never dull.

In 1871, however, Edison found that instead of working on new inventions, he was constantly thinking about the shy and beautiful Mary Sitwell, a sixteen-year-old girl who had come to work at the laboratory. He married her on Christmas Day, 1871, and set up home in a house in Newark that he had bought just a few days earlier.

Even on his wedding day, Edison insisted on going in to his lab to work on a few problems. This set the pattern for their married life. In the Edison household 'Father's work always came first.' As a family joke, the two oldest Edison children, Marion, born in 1872, and Thomas, born in 1876, were nicknamed Dot and Dash after the Morse code signals. His third child, William Leslie, born in 1878, had to make do with his own name!

Edison married Mary Sitwell on Christmas Day, 1871. Even on his wedding day, Edison could not resist going into his laboratory to work.

Edison's years at Newark were happy and productive. He set aside a room on the top floor of the Newark workshop as his own laboratory, and there he was able to work on his inventions to his heart's content. In 1872 and 1873, he patented sixty-three new inventions, and by 1878 he had taken out over 200 patents. Edison soon gained a reputation as a young wonder, who could sort out problems in almost any kind of machine. Before long, companies were bringing their problems to the young inventor, to see if he could solve them.

One of the first major projects at Newark concerned improvements to an automatic telegraph machine, which had been invented by a man named George D. Little. The invention had been bought by a newly-formed company, called the Automatic Telegraph Company, which discovered that the machine did not work well over distances of more than 320 kilometres. The company hoped Edison could improve it.

Edison's first step was to find out all he could about how the machine worked. In six weeks Edison read through a huge pile of chemistry books and performed 2,000 experiments. He also found the answer to the problem. The trouble turned out to be at the receiving end, which was affected by electrostatic interference, which meant that the incoming signals were 'smeared' or poorly defined. Edison found that by using a coil of wire wrapped around a soft iron bar, he was able to produce a momentary reversal of current at the end of each impulse. This meant that each signal could be very sharply defined. In his test runs, he found he could transmit over 1,000 words per minute in Morse code. The fastest telegraphers could transmit only about 45 words per minute.

An operator using a train telegraph. Telegraphers could transmit up to about 45 words per minute, but with his new invention Edison found he could transmit over 1,000 words per minute.

In 1873 and 1874, Edison was engrossed in improving his duplex telegraph. As more and more messages were being sent by telegraph, it became urgent to find ways of handling the increasing traffic. Both Western Union and the Automatic Telegraph Company agreed to give Edison some money to work on the telegraph. Western Union also agreed to let him use their lines for experiments after hours.

New York in the 1890s. The telegraph wires shown at the top of the picture represented an important means of communication in this busy commercial centre.

The quadruplex telegraph

The old duplex telegraph could send two messages at once, but only in opposite directions. It did this by using a neutral relay, which varied the strength of the electric current sent down the wire. Edison's first improvement was to invent the diplex telegraph, which could send two messages simultaneously in the same direction over one wire. To accomplish this, Edison added a polarized relay, which responded only to changes in the direction of the current passing through it. By using a 'pole changer' in place of the regular sending key, he could bring about instantaneous reversals in the direction of flow of the current.

By combining the duplex and the diplex systems, Edison was able to invent a quadruplex system, which could send four messages, two in one direction, and two in the opposite direction, at the same time. This greatly increased the number of messages that could be sent and received by telegraph offices like the one below.

In time, Edison invented a quadruplex telegraph – one that could manage successfully two outgoing and two incoming messages at the same time. This complex invention applied electricity in a revolutionary way, and won Edison the respect of the scientific community. It was also the cause of a bitter lawsuit between Western Union and the Automatic Telegraph Company over who owned the rights to the invention. Neither company thought to pay Edison for the invention, but he did not care.

In the spring of 1876, Edison set up a new laboratory in the small town of Menlo Park, New Jersey. Many of his assistants from Newark came, too, and the atmosphere in the laboratory was happy and unconventional. There was a lot of laughter, joking and teasing at the new laboratory, but a lot of hard work, too. Their stated production target was to produce a minor invention every ten days, and a major one every six months.

Edison's Menlo Park laboratory in the winter of 1879.

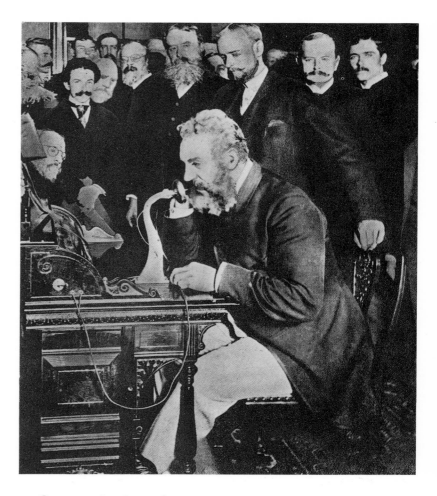

One of the first projects at Menlo Park concerned acoustic telegraphy. Edison had already begun experimenting with sound waves when Alexander Graham Bell invented the first telephone in 1876.

At first, the telegraph companies dismissed the telephone as unimportant. The president of Western Union called it an electrical toy. But once Western Union realized that this 'toy' could turn out to be a threat to its telegraph service, the Company asked Edison to try to come up with an improved version. Surprisingly, Edison's deafness proved to be an advantage for this project. Because he could not hear very well himself, he was determined that his telephone should have the clearest possible sound.

T E L E P H O N E.

PLATE 1

Graham Bell's first telephone.   *Transmitter.*   *Receiver.*

Instruments Exhibited at Philadelphia in 1876.

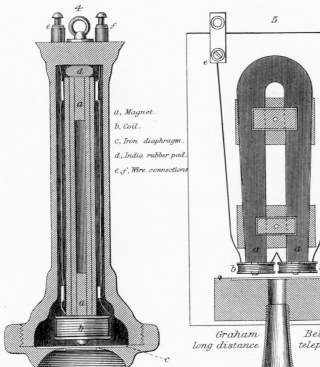

a, Magnet.

b, Coil.

c, Iron diaphragm.

d, India rubber pad.

e f, Wire connections

Graham Bell's hand telephone.

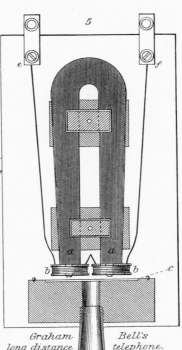

Graham Bell's long distance telephone.

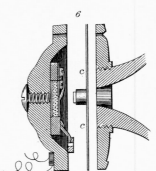

Section of Edison's Transmitter.

Edison's Transmitter.

a, Carbon. b, Vulcanite ring. c, diaphragm.

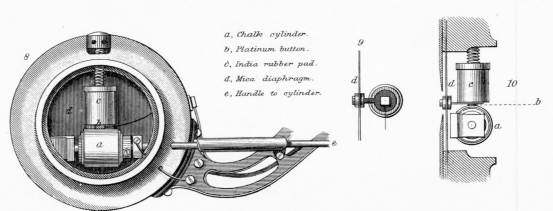

a, Chalk cylinder.

b, Platinum button.

c, India rubber pad.

d, Mica diaphragm.

e, Handle to cylinder.

Receiver of Edison's Loud speaking Telephone.

Opposite *The Bell and Edison telephones compared.*

An improved telephone

In Bell's telephone the same instrument acted as a transmitter and a receiver. Vibrations made by the human voice induced electrical impulses. These electrical impulses travelled along wires and were reproduced as sounds at the other end. The problem was that the sounds were very faint, especially over long distances.

Edison's telephone had a separate transmitter and receiver. To transmit the sounds, the voice caused a valve to open and close. The valve regulated the current, and reproduced the sounds much more clearly.

But Edison was not satisfied. He wanted to develop a better transmitter to reproduce sounds more clearly over long distances. Edison and his assistants tried nearly 2,000 substances before they eventually discovered that a plug of carbon 'gave splendid results' (see opposite). A version of Edison's carbon button transmitter is used in modern telephones – the picture below shows a man using a car phone.

One of Edison's first sketches for his phonograph.

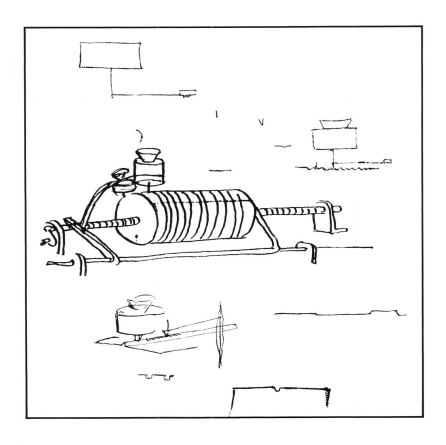

Edison working on his phonograph in the laboratory.

Working on the telephone gave Edison the idea of inventing a machine that would repeat the sound of the human voice. After months of work, Edison presented a sketch of the new machine to one of his assistants, and asked him to build it. 'What's this machine for, anyway?' the assistant asked. 'If it goes right, it might just repeat my voice when I speak into it,' Edison replied. The assistant thought the idea was absurd, and even Edison himself had his doubts about whether it would work, but he was determined to try.

The machine had a slender cylinder set on a long shaft, which was turned by a hand crank. A sheet of tinfoil was wrapped around the cylinder. When Edison spoke into the machine he turned the hand crank. This made the cylinder rotate and caused the pin to make a spiral groove in the disc which matched his voice.

All the lab workers gathered on the evening of 4 December 1877, to see the first trial run. As Edison turned the handle he said 'Mary had a little lamb'. When Edison attached a second pin to a second disc and turned the handle, the pin picked up the voice pattern on the tinfoil and turned it into vibrations which produced the sound. The words 'Mary had a little lamb' came from the machine. It worked! The laboratory spent the rest of the night excitedly trying out the new invention.

Edison called his new machine the phonograph, from the Greek words 'phono' for sound, and 'graph' for writing (today we call it the gramophone or record player, but Edison's machine could both record and play back sounds). When he announced his new invention to the world he became a celebrity overnight. 'I've made a good many machines,' Edison said, 'but this is my baby and I expect it to grow up and be a big feller, and support me in my old age.'

The phonograph has changed greatly since its invention, as this twin deck record player shows.

In 1878, people still lit their houses with gas and oil lamps. After his great success with the phonograph, Edison decided to change all that. He set himself the task of developing a 'safe, mild and inexpensive' form of electric lighting that people could use in their houses.

The idea of electric lighting was not new. In 1810, Sir Humphry Davy had demonstrated to the Royal Institution in London that it was possible to produce light by making an electric current jump between two carbon rods, or electrodes. This electric arc lighting was beginning to be used for street lighting in some large cities. But it was smelly, produced a harsh glare and needed constant attention to keep it running. It also used a lot of electric current, and the lamps were connected in series. This meant that the electric current flowed from one lamp to another, and if one lamp in the series went out or was turned off, all the other lights went out too.

In a series circuit, electrical current flows from one electric lamp to the next. If one lamp burns out, all the other lamps go out too. In a parallel circuit, the current is divided so that each lamp receives only a fraction of the total current. Individual lamps can be turned off without affecting the other lamps in the circuit.

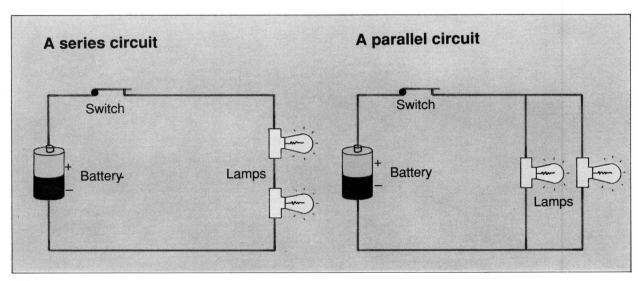

A series circuit   **A parallel circuit**

Switch   Switch

Battery   Lamps   Battery

Lamps

Edison experimenting with carbonized paper during his search for a suitable filament to use in his electric light bulb.

Edison saw that it would be better to use a parallel circuit for lighting. In a parallel circuit, the current is divided so that each light receives only a fraction of the total current, and it can be turned off without affecting the other lights. Rather than powering electric lighting using a dynamo in each individual home, as some people had proposed, Edison had the idea of setting up a central electricity power station, which could feed energy into buildings by means of wires. By measuring the amount of current that went into each building, people could be charged for the electricity they used.

The first problem was to find a light bulb which would run on low currents. Edison saw that, in theory, an incandescent lamp – one with a filament or thin strand of carbon sealed in an airless glass chamber – had the right sort of properties. The filament would heat up and give off light when an electric current was passed through it. But, in practice, it was much more difficult to produce an incandescent bulb than Edison thought. It turned out to be very difficult to make a filament that would burn for more than a few minutes. The filament has to be very thin in order to be able to heat up using only the small currents but, because it is so thin, it breaks easily. In addition, it proved very difficult to produce a vacuum cheaply and easily inside the glass bulb – when the filament is exposed to oxygen in the air, it burns quickly.

Edison testing incandescent light bulbs in his Menlo Park laboratory.

A diagram, first published in 1879 in the magazine Scientific American, *showing Edison's incandescent lamp.*

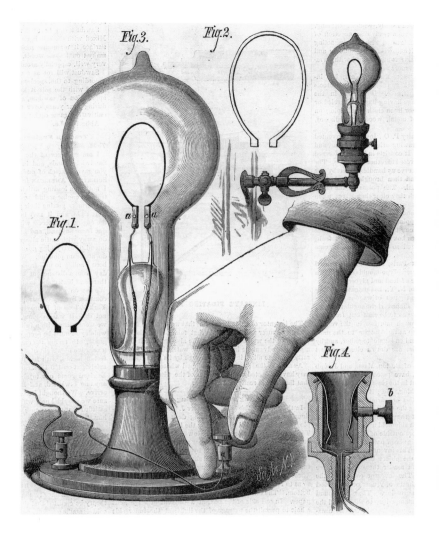

Edison knew that he would have to work hard to come up with the answer, and he also knew that he would need money to pay for the research. One of Edison's early ideas was to use platinum for the filament. This burned for longer than carbon, but still not long enough. Nevertheless, Edison encouraged newspapers to report on his latest 'success' in order to attract financial backers for his scheme. Investors were persuaded to invest in a system not yet invented because Edison had a wonderful record of past achievements. In 1878, with the help of rich and powerful investors, Edison was able to set up the Edison Electric Light Company to support his research.

Although the newspapers proclaimed that the platinum filament was a success, Edison knew that it was not the answer. But what was the solution? Edison was determined to find out, no matter how many materials he had to test. One of his assistants claimed that if Edison had to find a needle in a haystack, he would examine straw after straw until he found the needle. Edison himself put it another way. He said that genius was the result of 1 per cent inspiration, and 99 per cent perspiration!

The first breakthrough came when Edison heard of a new type of vacuum pump, which made it possible to remove almost all of the air from inside the bulbs. In October 1879, Edison discovered that, after all, a thin thread of carbon made the best filament, and he soon found out how to make carbon threads that would burn for 170 hours. At about the same time, an English

Edison designed his electrical lighting system to be powered from a central generator. The picture shows the interior of an Edison electricity generating plant in Paris in 1887.

inventor, Joseph Swan, had also come up with a carbon filament bulb, and eventually the two inventors joined forces to form a joint lighting company. Just after Christmas, 1879, Edison demonstrated the new lighting system to the press, and newspaper headlines were soon proclaiming that the lighting of the future had arrived.

But Edison was not finished yet. He wanted to develop a complete electric light system powered from a central generator. He decided to establish the first light and power system in New York and, in 1881, set up a headquarters on Fifth Avenue, right in the heart of the city. There were many practical, as well as political, problems to overcome. The gas companies regarded the new electric lighting and power system as a threat to their business and did their best to place obstacles in the way.

Today, electric lights make streets bright at night.

The Edison effect

During the course of his work on electric lights, Edison accidentally discovered what became known as the Edison effect. He found that by connecting a second filament to the positive side of the electric circuit within a light bulb, a current flowed within the bulb. Although Edison did not fully understand this effect, he was convinced it would be useful and patented it. It turned out to be the forerunner of the electronic tube.

Discovery of the Edison effect opened up the whole new world of electronics, and inventions such as radio, television, computers (below) and radar depended on it. The electronic tubes have now been replaced by transistors, but when they were invented they were revolutionary. The discovery of the Edison effect made Edison 'the father of modern electronics'.

Edison opened his first power plant at Pearl Street in New York on 4 September 1882. He purposely switched on the power during daylight, so that if anything went wrong with the lights it would not be very obvious. But nothing did go wrong, and by nightfall Edison's electric light and power business was serving eighty-five satisfied customers. Even though there were still some problems to be worked out, people gradually began switching to the new electric lights.

In 1884, when Edison was at the height of his fame, his wife, Mary, died suddenly of typhoid fever. Edison was heartbroken. After Mary's death he decided that he never wanted to see their home in Menlo Park again. Edison took his

Edison (right) in his workshop listening to an improved version of his phonograph.

children to live in New York and threw himself once again into his work to try to forget his sorrow. In 1885 Edison fell in love with a beautiful eighteen-year-old girl named Mina Miller. Before long they were married and, eventually, had three children.

Edison's second wife, Mina Miller, whom he married in 1885.

In 1887, Edison and his young wife moved to West Orange, New Jersey. Here, Edison set up an even bigger laboratory than the one he had built in Menlo Park, and began work again. He first turned his attention to the phonograph and it was not long before he came up with an improved version which used a wax cylinder, rather than one made out of tinfoil.

In 1912, Edison combined his kinetoscope, a type of moving picture camera, with his phonograph to make the first 'talking pictures'.

He also invented the kinetoscope, a type of camera which recorded pictures of objects in motion and 'did for the eye, what the phonograph did for the ear'. This was the beginning of cinema or motion pictures. In 1912, he combined the kinetoscope with the phonograph to make the first 'talking pictures', and by tinting each frame with a special paint, made the first colour film.

Ever anxious for new challenges, Edison now turned his attention to developing a battery. This battery eventually proved useful as a back-up source of power for power plants and also for railway signalling. It was used to provide electricity on ships during the First World War (1914–18), and was the first type of battery to power naval torpedoes.

A modern film set. Edison's kinetoscope was the forerunner of today's cine-camera.

7 Inventing the Future

When the USA entered the First World War in 1917, Edison was seventy years old. Although he considered himself to be a pacifist, Edison used his skills to help the American war effort by working on naval weapons. Whenever he could, he worked on devices that would be used for defence, rather than attack, and on systems such as underwater telephone lines, which could be used during peacetime.

Edison working in his laboratory.

Thomas Edison had seen great changes during his lifetime, and many of these changes had been due to his own inventions. When he was born, people lit their houses with candles and oil lamps. By the end of his life, many houses were lit with electric light. Cinemas provided entertainment, Edison's phonograph brought pleasure to many, and his improved telephone meant long distance communication was open to everyone. Edison was a popular figure; his assistants loved and respected him, and he was always happy to show people around his laboratories. This open and enthusiastic attitude did much to create a public interest in science.

In 1927, Edison celebrated the fiftieth anniversary of his invention of the phonograph by broadcasting 'Mary had a little lamb', a repeat of the first sentence he recorded on his original invention.

Henry Ford (left) with Edison (third left) and the President of the United States, Herbert Hoover (second right), at Dearborn, Michigan, in 1929.

In 1928 the United States Congress summed up the feelings of the world when they presented the great inventor with a gold medal for his inventions which 'revolutionized civilization'. In 1929, President Hoover gave a banquet in honour of Edison and to commemorate the fiftieth anniversary of the invention of the light bulb. During this banquet Edison suffered an attack of a kidney disease and collapsed.

Although very ill, Edison lived for another two years. He remained active and curious, and from his home in New Jersey he followed new technological advances and studied complex problems such as the use of atomic energy.

When Edison died on 18 October 1931, telegraph, telephone, radio and newsreels relayed the sad news around the world. At 10 pm on the day of his funeral, people all over the USA, including the President, turned off the electric lights in their houses as a tribute to his achievements. Even the torch on the Statue of Liberty went out. Once more the night was dark, just as it had been when Edison was born. One minute later the lights came on, and the race towards the future, in which Edison had played such a prominent part, was on again.

Date Chart

1847 11 February. Thomas Alva Edison born in Milan, Ohio, USA.

1862–8 Works as a telegraph operator.

1868 Moves to Boston. Invents the automatic vote recorder.

1869 Moves to New York. With two partners establishes Pope, Edison and Company, the first electrical engineering company in the USA.

1870 Edison sets up in business on his own.

1871 Marries Mary Sitwell.

1876 Invents the carbon button transmitter to improve the quality of sound on telephones. Establishes a laboratory in Menlo Park, New Jersey.

1877 Invents the phonograph.

1879 31 December. Exhibits an electric lighting system at the Menlo Park laboratories.

1881 Opens offices in New York and establishes the first commercial manufacture of incandescent lamps.

1882 4 September. Opens the first commercial central electric lighting station in the USA at 255–257 Pearl Street, New York.

1883 Patents the Edison effect.

1884 Mary Edison dies.

1885 Marries Mina Miller.

1887 Moves his laboratory to West Orange, New Jersey.

1891 Invents the kinetoscope, a type of motion picture camera.

1912 Combines the kinetoscope with the phonograph to make the first 'talking pictures'.

1928 The US Congress presents Edison with a gold medal for 'inventions which revolutionized civilization'.

1931 18 October. Edison dies.

Books to Read

Thomas Edison, Genius of Electricity by Keith Ellis (Wayland, 1977)
Thomas Edison: The Great American Inventor by Louise Eagan (Barron's Educational Series, 1987)
Thomas Edison by Josephine Ross (Hamish Hamilton, 1982)
Thomas Edison by Richard Tames (Franklin Watts, 1990)
Thomas Edison by Theodore Rowland-Entwistle (Cherrytree Press, 1988)

Glossary

Acoustic Of or related to hearing or sound.

Civil War The war fought between the southern states of America, which favoured slavery, and the northern states which wanted to see slavery abolished. It was fought between 1861 and 1865.

Conductor A substance or device that is used to transmit electricity or heat.

Dynamo A device for generating electricity.

Electrical engineering Designing and building machines which use electricity.

Electric circuit An arrangement of wires through which electrical current travels.

Electrode A conductor through which electricity enters or leaves.

Electromagnetic impulse A pulse of electric current created through the use of magnets and coils of wire.

Electronic tubes Vacuum tubes in which the negatively charged electrons released from a hot filament are attracted to a positively charged plate. The electronic tube is based on the Edison effect. Its development led to many useful inventions, such as X-ray tubes, radios and radar.

Electrostatic interference Interference caused by electrical charges which are at rest, or not moving.

Generator A device for producing electricity.

Incandescence Bright light produced by the glowing of a white-hot filament.

Neutral relay A kind of switch that allows a weak current to open and close a circuit in which a stronger current flows.

Parallel circuit An electrical circuit where components are arranged so that the same electrical force is applied to each. In a parallel lighting circuit, if one bulb burns out, the rest will still shine.

Patent A legal document which gives the inventor the sole right to make, use or sell his invention.

Polarized relay A type of switch that responds only to changes in the direction of the electric current passing through it.

Receiver A device for changing variations in electrical current into sound vibrations.

Series circuit An electrical circuit where the same current flows in turn through each of the components. In a lighting circuit arranged in series, if one bulb burns out, all the bulbs will go out.

Picture Acknowledgements

Mary Evans *cover*, 5 (top), 10, 11, 13, 14, 17, 18, 19, 22, 23, 25, 34, 36, 40, 41, 45; Billie Love Collection 4; Mansell Collection iii, 7, 9, 15, 24, 27, 28, 30, (lower) 33, 35, 43; Topham 5 (lower), 31, 37, 42, 44; Wayland Picture Library 6, 12, 16, 21, 26, 30 (top), 39; Zefa 29, 38. Illustrations: cover artwork by Richard Hook; Jenny Hughes 8, 32.

Index

48